Lectionary Tales For The Pulpit

Series II
Cycle C

Written and Compiled
by
John R. Steward

CSS Publishing Company, Inc., Lima, Ohio

LECTIONARY TALES FOR THE PULPIT, SERIES II, CYCLE C

Copyright © 1997 by
CSS Publishing Company, Inc.
Lima, Ohio

All rights reserved. No part of this publication may be reproduced in any manner whatsoever without the prior permission of the publisher, except in the case of brief quotations embodied in critical articles and reviews. Inquiries should be addressed to: Permissions, CSS Publishing Company, Inc., P.O. Box 4503, Lima, Ohio 45802-4503.

Scripture quotations are from the *Revised Standard Version of the Bible*, copyrighted 1946, 1952 (c), 1971, 1973, by the Division of Christian Education of the National Council of the Churches of Christ in the USA. Used by permission.

Library of Congress Cataloging-in-Publication Data

Steward, John R.
   Lectionary tales for the pulpit. Series II. Cycle C / John R. Steward.
      p.   cm.
   Includes bibliographical references.
   ISBN 0-7880-1056-5 (pbk.)
   1. Lectionary preaching. 2. Homiletical illustrations. I. Title.
BV4235.L43S74   1997
252'.6—dc21   96-52621
                                                                                     CIP

In remembrance of my late father, Warren C. Steward, who encouraged me in telling the stories of God's Word.

Table Of Contents

Introduction — 9

1. **Advent 1** — 11
   1 Thessalonians 3:9-13

2. **Advent 2** — 12
   Luke 3:1-6

3. **Advent 3** — 13
   Luke 3:7-18

4. **Advent 4** — 15
   Luke 1:39-45

5. **Christmas 1** — 16
   Colossians 3:12-17

6. **Epiphany Of The Lord** — 18
   Matthew 2:1-12

7. **Baptism Of The Lord** — 20
   Acts 8:14-17

8. **Epiphany 2** — 21
   John 2:1-11

9. **Epiphany 3** — 23
   1 Corinthians 12:12-31a

10. **Epiphany 4** — 25
    1 Corinthians 13:1-13

11. **Epiphany 5** — 26
    Luke 5:1-11

12. **Epiphany 6**   28
   1 Corinthians 15:12-20

13. **Transfiguration Sunday**   29
   2 Corinthians 3:12—4:2

14. **Lent 1**   30
   Romans 10:8b-13

15. **Lent 2**   31
   Luke 13:31-35

16. **Lent 3**   32
   Luke 13:1-9

17. **Lent 4**   34
   2 Corinthians 5:16-21

18. **Lent 5**   36
   Philippians 3:4b-14

19. **Passion/Palm Sunday**   37
   Philippians 2:5-11

20. **Easter**   38
   1 Corinthians 15:19-26

21. **Easter 2**   40
   John 20:19-31

22. **Easter 3**   42
   John 21:1-19

23. **Easter 4**   44
   Revelation 7:9-17

24. **Easter 5**   45
   John 13:31-35

25. **Easter 6**   46
   John 14:23-29

26.	**Ascension Sunday** Luke 24:44-53	48
27.	**Day Of Pentecost** John 14:8-17 (25-27)	49
28.	**Trinity Sunday** John 16:12-15	51
29.	**Proper 6** Luke 7:36—8:3	52
30.	**Proper 7** Galatians 3:23-29	53
31.	**Proper 8** Galatians 5:1, 13-25	54
32.	**Proper 9** Galatians 6:7-16	56
33.	**Proper 10** Luke 10:25-37	57
34.	**Proper 11** Luke 10:38-42	59
35.	**Proper 12** Colossians 2:6-15	60
36.	**Proper 13** Luke 12:13-21	61
37.	**Proper 14** Hebrews 11:1-3, 8-16	62
38.	**Proper 15** Hebrews 11:29—12:2	63
39.	**Proper 16** Hebrews 12:18-29	65

40.	**Proper 17** Hebrews 13:1-8, 15-16	66
41.	**Proper 18** Luke 14:25-33	67
42.	**Proper 19** Luke 15:1-10	69
43.	**Proper 20** 1 Timothy 2:1-7	70
44.	**Proper 21** 1 Timothy 6:6-19	71
45.	**Proper 22** 2 Timothy 1:1-14	73
46.	**Proper 23** Luke 17:11-19	74
47.	**Proper 24** 2 Timothy 3:14—4:5	75
48.	**Proper 25** 2 Timothy 4:6-8, 16-18	77
49.	**All Saints' Day** Ephesians 1:11-23	79
50.	**Proper 27** 2 Thessalonians 2:1-5, 13-17	81
51.	**Proper 28** 2 Thessalonians 3:6-13	82
52.	**Christ The King** Luke 23:33-43	84

Topical Index — 85

Scriptural Index — 87

Introduction

How many times has a pastor been looking for a story that would best illustrate the theme of the text from which the pastor is preaching? It is very frustrating. The pastor looks through recent periodicals and devotional books, unable to find that one story that will really capture the imagination of the listening audience. Unable to find anything suitable, the pastor continues to write a sermon that is not everything he or she wanted it to be. The congregation may never know the difference, but the pastor does.

This is an attempt to help the pastor in just such a situation. After many years of preaching and teaching, I, too, have run into this situation on more than one occasion. I have tried to find the best stories I can and to match them with the pericopes for each Sunday in the church year. These are stories that have intrigue, creativity, and often a twist at the end. These are stories that are meant to enhance the text for the day in such a way that the congregants will leave remembering the major theme of the sermon. These are not just a group of stories but rather true examples from history and fiction with imagination and excitement.

These stories, however, are not just for pastors writing sermons, but also for lay people who give Bible studies at their churches. Sunday school teachers will find these stories also to be very helpful in their classes. Even the average business speaker will find stories that will help make the points he or she is emphasizing in his presentation. A handy index will help everyone find the right story listed under the various subject and topic headings.

I believe that stories are a vital form of communication. If people have been listening to a sermon or a lecture and find that they are daydreaming, they will always be brought back to the presentation with a story. If it is a good story, they will remember it and think about the point you have made. Stories help people to become involved in what you are talking about. They become caught up in the story and even see themselves in the events of the story. When that happens in a sermon, a person is actually experiencing, in a personal way, the sermon.

The greatest indicator that stories should be used in sermons and other forms of communicating the Gospel is that Jesus himself used stories. Whenever he wanted to reach a large variety of people, he would tell a story in the form of a parable. All people could see themselves in the stories that Jesus told. His stories had life-changing impact and still do. I pray that these stories will help you tell the Gospel story.

A special thank you to my patient and loving wife Torild and to my children Sean and Astrid. Their support has been very meaningful in this project. Thank you to Betsy Dubow for going the extra mile in the accomplishment of this work. And last, but not least, we give thanks and praise to the Lord of the Church whose Gospel story we are attempting to tell.

1

Advent 1
1 Thessalonians 3:9-13

"And may the Lord make you increase and abound in love to one another and to all men, as we do to you...." (v. 12)

What is love? It is difficult for most people to define love very well other than it is a feeling that they experience. Someone has said that love is a verb. That is what Beno Fischer found out many years ago.

Beno Fischer is a survivor of the Nazi concentration camps of World War II. During that terrible ordeal, Beno encountered a man who begged him to "trade my cold soup for his cube of bread." He really did not want to do it because he himself was very hungry. But it was apparent that this other man was near death. Even though the cold soup would have satisfied Beno's hunger more than the dry bread, he made the trade anyway. "Each day I set the tasteless broth by his bedside and slowly bit off pieces of the bland crust of bread."

When the camp was finally liberated, the captives were taken to a hospital and given physical examinations. Beno says, "The doctor told me I lived for only one reason: out of love for my fellow prisoner, I traded my soup for the bread! The bread had enough nutrition in it to keep me alive. The soup had no source of nourishment."

Perhaps then, the best definition of love is in learning how to forget and abandon ourselves and to serve others. At least that is what we find in Jesus Christ.

Source: Robert Schuller, *It's Possible* (Old Tappan, New Jersey: Fleming H. Revell Company), p. 99.

2

Advent 2
Luke 3:1-6

While Khrushchev was Premier of the Soviet Union, he came out against his predecessor Joseph Stalin and his abuses of power. As he was giving his speech denouncing Stalin, someone in the Congress Hall shouted, "Where were you, Comrade Khrushchev, when all these innocent people were being slaughtered?"

At that moment there was total silence as everyone wondered what would happen next. Khrushchev stopped speaking and began looking around the hall. He said, "Will the man who said that kindly stand up?"

No one stood up. Everyone was frozen in his seat.

Khrushchev then said, "Well, whoever you are, you have your answer now. I was in exactly the same position then as you are now."

John the Baptist was not afraid to speak up. John the Baptist was not afraid to tell the people of his day to "prepare the way of the Lord."

Source: *The Pastor's Story File* (P.O. Box 8, Platteville, Colorado 80651-0008: Saratoga Press 303-785-2990), May 1992 issue. Used by permission.

3

Advent 3
Luke 3:7-18

When the Gettysburg Cemetery was being dedicated, those doing the planning wanted to have a speaker whom everyone would know. They wanted a speaker who would draw a crowd. They chose none other than Edward Everett, who was extremely well-known and respected. If they had a man like Edward Everett, they knew for sure that the event would be a great success. The planning committee would not have to worry about the event and they were certain that the ceremony would be a sterling success.

However, when they extended the official invitation they ran into a problem. Edward Everett would not be able to speak on that particular date. So the decision was made to change the date of the ceremony to accommodate the great speaker Edward Everett. When the decision was made, Edward Everett was able to accept the invitation.

They also extended another invitation. They invited the President of the United States, Abraham Lincoln, to speak as well.

On November 19, 1864, Edward Everett spoke for nearly two hours. The crowd that was gathered was thrilled that such a famous orator would be their keynote speaker. When Everett concluded his speech, Abraham Lincoln took the stage and spoke for only a couple of minutes. His address contained only 267 words structured in only ten sentences. These words have remained in the conscience of Americans ever since: "That government of the people, by the people, for the people shall not perish from the earth." And perhaps because he was a great orator, it was Edward Everett who took Lincoln's hand and said, "My speech will soon be forgotten; yours never will be. How gladly would I exchange my hundred pages for your twenty lines." Today we still remember Lincoln's words and no one can even tell you who Edward Everett is or what he did that great day at Gettysburg.

Perhaps this helps us to understand the circumstances surrounding John the Baptist. Perhaps we can better comprehend these words from Luke's gospel when he writes: "As the people were in expectation, and all men questioned in their hearts concerning John, whether perhaps he were the Christ, John answered them all, 'I baptize you with water, but he who is mightier than I is coming, the thong of whose sandals I am not worthy to untie; he will baptize you with the Holy Spirit and with fire.' "

Source: Paul Boller, *Presidential Anecdotes* (New York City: Penguin Books), p. 129.

4

Advent 4
Luke 1:39-45

My friend, Pastor Ray Christenson in Las Vegas, once told about a pastor who would regularly visit a farm family outside of town. He would visit them particularly because the farmer's wife was blind. Each time the pastor would visit, things would go along like any of the other visits he would make. He enjoyed talking with Farmer and Mrs. Syverson. They would tell the pastor of how their families came from Norway and how they settled in Minnesota. They would share their remembrances of family traditions and customs. It was always an enjoyable time together. The pastor would then try to direct the visit toward spiritual matters. He would offer to pray or to share Holy Communion. During these moments the farmer would excuse himself and go outside to continue his chores around the farm. When this happened, the pastor noticed something that he could never understand.

As the farmer would work around the farm, the pastor noticed that he always whistled. In and of itself, this was not very strange. What was odd was that it was never a tune that the pastor could recognize. So on one of those many visits, as the pastor got in his car to drive back to town, he gathered the courage to ask the farmer about his whistling. "Mr. Syverson," he asked, "I notice that when I am visiting with your wife, you are out here working, and while you do, you are whistling, but it is never a tune I recognize. What are you whistling?" "Pastor," the farmer replied, "you know that my wife is blind and while I am out here working, I whistle so that she will know that I am near."

God became a man in Jesus Christ so that we would know that he is near. He comes to us in such simple ways. He comes to us even as a little baby. Listen for the whistling of God.

Source: Ray Christenson, Community Lutheran Church, Las Vegas, Nevada. Used by permission.

5

Christmas 1
Colossians 3:12-17

A farmer was being questioned by a lawyer during a trial concerning an accident on a highway. The lawyer asked the farmer, "Is it true, Mr. Jones, that when the highway patrol officer came over to you after the accident, you said, 'I feel fine'?"

Farmer Jones began to answer by saying, "Well, now, me and my cow Bessie were driving down the highway in my pickup truck when ..." At this point the attorney interrupted, saying, "Please just answer my question with a yes or a no; did you say to the officer, 'I feel fine'?" Farmer Jones then tried to answer the question again. He said, "Well, now, me and my cow Bessie were driving down the highway in my pickup truck when ..." The attorney stopped him again and this time asked the judge to intervene. He said, "Your honor, would you please instruct the witness to simply answer my question with a yes or a no." The judge said, "Why don't we just let him tell his story?"

So, Farmer Jones told his story. "Me and my cow Bessie were driving down the highway in my pickup truck. Bessie, of course, was in the bed of the truck. I heard a loud bang and knew that I had blown out a tire. The truck went flying off the road and landed in a ditch. I went flying out of the truck on one side of the highway and Bessie landed on the other side. When I woke up, the highway patrol officer came over to me and said that Bessie was in awful shape. He then went back over to Bessie, pulled out his gun and shot her dead. Then he came over to me and asked me how I felt and I said, " 'I feel fine, just fine.' "

Fear causes us to do things and say things that we might not do otherwise. Fear can be a powerful motivator in our lives. Too often fear is a destructive force with little redeeming value. In this scripture reading, the Apostle Paul encourages us to "let the peace of Christ rule in your hearts...." He even goes on to say that we have been called to this experience of peace in Jesus Christ. We were built and designed by God to be a people of faith, not fear. Faith in the one who redeems us will lead to peace.

Source: *Parables, Etc.* (Platteville, Colorado: Saratoga Press), October 1991. Used by permission.

6

Epiphany Of The Lord
Matthew 2:1-12

Many years ago there was a play named *Eagerheart*. It told of a young peasant girl by the name of Eagerheart who lived in the country. She was a very attractive girl who lived in a small hut.

One day the news was being spread that the King of England was coming for a visit. Eagerheart was very excited about this news. This was a once in a lifetime opportunity to see the King. On the day that the King was to arrive, another peasant woman, partially covered with a shawl, arrived at Eagerheart's hut with a baby in her arms, asking for lodging. She said that she had been traveling a long way and needed a place to stay for a night with the baby. Eagerheart had compassion for the woman and let her into her hut. She explained that she was "in a hurry to leave and that she had to get to town." With that announcement she was out the door and on her way to see the King.

On her way she encountered three Oriental men who were holding some very expensive gifts. They asked her for help to find their way. After she gave them directions, they explained their purpose. They told her that they had special information that the King was coming. Eagerheart said, "I know, that's why I'm going to the village." The men told her that the special information that they had indicated that they must go to the countryside to find the King. She did not want to argue with them and so she continued on her way. When she got to the village the people were pouring out of the town. She asked someone where they were going. He answered by saying, "The King is coming, and the word is that he's out in the country."

Eagerheart decided that she would follow along with the rest of the crowd. As they got farther and farther away from the village, she noticed that they were getting closer and closer to her little hut. Finally, she noticed a large group of people in front of her hut and she said, "He can't be in there, that is my place!" But when she went inside, she found that same woman she had let into her home. When the woman stood and removed her shawl, Eagerheart knew immediately that it was the queen mother of England and that the baby was indeed the King of England.

Overwhelmed, Eagerheart said, "Oh, had I stayed home, I could have spent the time alone with him!" But then she concluded, "At least I gave him the best that I had."

Source: Robert Schuller, *Be an Extraordinary Person in an Ordinary World* (Old Tappan, New Jersey: Fleming H. Revell Company), p. 112.

7

Baptism Of The Lord
Acts 8:14-17

"Then they [Peter and John] laid their hands on them and they received the Holy Spirit. Now when Simon saw that the Spirit was given through the laying on of the apostles' hands, he offered them money, saying, 'Give me also this power....'" (vv. 17-19a)

Many years ago the founder and president of the National Cash Register Company of Dayton, Ohio, used a similar technique in motivating people. Mr. Patterson would choose some of his up-and-coming young executives and tell them to take their wives to New York City on company expense. He would tell them to stay at the finest hotel in the city and to go to the best restaurants. They were encouraged to go shopping for the wives to buy new clothes or anything else that they might like to have. They were invited to go to a Broadway show while they were in the city. All this would be done at company expense. However, even though the National Cash Register Company would pay for all of this, Mr. Patterson had a reason. Mr. Patterson believed that once his employees and their wives experienced the finer things of life, they would come back wanting to earn more money, which would cause them to work even harder and be of a greater value to the company.

This might work in the business world, but Simon found out that it would never work in the Kingdom of God. "Peter said to him, 'Your silver perish with you, because you thought you could obtain the gift of God with money! You have neither part nor lot in this matter, for your heart is not right before God.'" God uses a different economy, and it is called grace. Those who have never experienced it will not understand it.

Source: Paul Strodach, *Calling All Christians* (Philadelphia: Muhlenberg Press).

8

Epiphany 2
John 2:1-11

When Theodore Roosevelt was an Assemblyman in the legislature of the state of New York, events developed in his personal life that would wound him deeply.

On February 13, Roosevelt, seated on the floor of the Assembly, received a telegram informing him that his wife Alice had given birth to a baby girl late the night before. He received the congratulations of his colleagues but decided to finish work on legislative matters before leaving for home to be with his family. Several hours later he received another telegram telling him that his wife was very ill and so too his mother. He immediately left for the train station.

The train seemed to move very slowly down the Hudson Valley. Normally, the trip took five hours but during this journey it would be longer due to the heavy fog. All Roosevelt could do was to read the two telegrams over and over again. When he finally did arrive at the station, it was difficult to find his home because of the fog. When he did find his home, he found that Alice, ill with Bright's disease, was semi-comatose and near death. Alice barely recognized him as he sat with her in his arms. Not only was his wife near death, but also his mother Mittie was dying with typhoid fever on the floor below.

Theodore Roosevelt was informed that if he wanted to see his mother for the last time he had better do that now. Finally, at three in the morning, Mittie died and Theodore went back upstairs to be with Alice. As morning came, the fog became even worse and then by mid-morning there was rain, which was eventually followed by a brief appearance of the sun. When the morning passed over into the afternoon, Alice died. It was February 14, 1884, and Roosevelt wrote in his diary: "The light was gone out of my life."

Two days after Alice's death, he wrote in his diary: "For joy or sorrow, my life has now been lived out."

Imagine, Theodore Roosevelt believed that his life was virtually over. He saw very little reason to go on with life. Yet this is the same man who would go on to be the President of the United States. As President, he would develop our national park system, develop laws against abusive child labor and laws to regulate the nation's food supply, develop the Panama Canal, and will always be remembered for the immortal words "speak softly and carry a big stick." Obviously, his life was not over when his mother and wife died.

Even at the marriage feast in Cana in Galilee, Jesus proved that God can do far more than we can ever anticipate. When we think that all hope is lost, God is still in the miracle business.

Source: Edmund Morris, *The Rise of Theodore Roosevelt* (New York City: Ballantine Books), pp. 24 and 240-245.

9

Epiphany 3
1 Corinthians 12:12-31a

"For just as the body is one and has many members, and all the members of the body, though many, are one body, so it is with Christ." (v. 12)

There was a man who had a dream one night that he had died. In his dream he found himself in a large room. The room had a very large banquet table filled with different kinds of food. There were people seated around the table but they were seated five feet away from the table. In his dream, the people were very hungry and wanted to eat but were unable to get out of their chairs. To make matters worse their arms were not long enough to be able to reach out and obtain the food.

As the man looked more closely, he saw a very large spoon that was five feet long that the people were fighting over for possession. In his dream, he watched with amazement how one person used the spoon to dish up some food and then carefully turned the spoon around toward his mouth with all the food falling off the spoon and onto the floor. Then another person grabbed the spoon but was unable to feed himself because of the length of the spoon.

Then the man turned to his guide and said: "This is hell; to have food and not be able to eat it." The guide replied, "Where do you think you are? This is hell. But this is not your place. Come with me." The guide took him to another room that was also filled with a large banquet table and delicious food. In this room, there was also a large spoon with a handle that was five feet long. However, in this room no one was fighting. Instead, one person would take the spoon and use it to feed another. They in turn would use the spoon to return the favor. The guide turned to the man and said, "This is heaven."

Source: Robert Schuller, *Be an Extraordinary Person in an Ordinary World* (Old Tappan, New Jersey: Fleming H. Revell Company), p. 113.

10

Epiphany 4
1 Corinthians 13:1-13

"Love does not insist on its own way; it is not irritable or resentful; it does not rejoice at wrong, but rejoices in the right." (vv. 5-6)

Andre Malraux, the French author, tells in his book *Lazarus* of being with the troops that liberated the Nazi extermination camps toward the end of World War II. He said that you could see the prisoners' skeletons through their skin. One journalist who was with the liberating troops was interviewing the now former prisoners. They were very weak and many were near death. The interviews did not last very long, but the power of what they said and the way they said it could not be measured by the length of the interview. One prisoner summed it up by simply saying, "You see, there's no room left in our hearts except for forgiveness."

The true language of love is forgiveness. Sometimes the only way we can forgive is to be so filled with the unconditional love of God that there is not room for anything else. The answer to our bitterness is to be filled with God's love in Jesus Christ.

Source: Andre Malraux, *Lazarus*.

11

Epiphany 5
Luke 5:1-11

"And Jesus said to Simon, 'Do not be afraid; henceforth you will be catching men.' " (v. 10)

So often we read these words of Jesus and wonder why we do not see this taking place in our churches. A few years ago, Dr. Win Arn did a survey of 1,000 congregations. The answers that he received might help us better understand the problem. He asked both the members and pastors of these churches what they thought the purpose of their church really was. Dr. Arn reports that 89 percent of the people in those churches said that the purpose of their church was to take care of the needs of the members. The remaining eleven percent believed that the purpose of the church was to reach the world with the gospel. Contrast this with the pastors. Ninety percent of the pastors said that the purpose of their church was to reach the world for Christ while the remaining ten percent of pastors in those churches agreed with the laity that the purpose of the church is to take care of the needs of the members of the church. Is it any wonder why there is conflict in our churches today?

The great Renaissance scholar Erasmus once told a very helpful mythical story. It seems that after Jesus returned to heaven the angels gathered around him. He told them about how on earth he had performed many miracles and how he spent time teaching the many who would come to him. He told them about his death, burial, and resurrection. He told them about his ascension to heaven. Then Michael the Archangel asked, "But Lord, what happens now?" Jesus answered by telling them that he had spent three years training his disciples to carry out his plan to reach the world with the gospel. He said, "I have left behind eleven faithful men who will declare my message and express my love. These faithful men will build my church." Then Michael asked: "What if these men fail? What then?" Then Jesus thought for a moment and said, "I have no other plan."

Source: Rick Warren, *The Purpose Driven Church* (Grand Rapids, Michigan: Zondervan Publishing House), p. 82.

Source: Tony Campolo, *Who Switched the Price Tags* (Dallas: Word Publishing), p. 170.

12

Epiphany 6
1 Corinthians 15:12-20

When I was in college my professor and good friend Dr. James Kallas would speak of the resurrection of Christ as being similar to the turning point in a war. He would use the Battle of the Bulge in World War II as an example. In recent years you could point to the Gulf War against Iraq. I remember how so many people predicted that this would be a very bloody war. They would point out how large Iraq's army was and that we should be prepared for many casualties coming home injured or in body bags. People were genuinely concerned and it was somewhat uncertain just how things would work out. Then the war began with the fighter jets bombing Iraq. In only two or three days, the Americans had obtained air superiority. When air superiority was achieved, there was no longer any doubt as to who the victor would be in that war. However, it was not at that moment when the war was over or when the killing would stop. It was the turning point in the war when we knew for certain who the victor would be in the end.

That is how it is with the resurrection of Jesus Christ. His resurrection is the turning point in the battle with "sin, death, and the power of the devil." We now know that, in the end, the ultimate victory is ours because of the resurrection of Jesus.

13

Transfiguration Sunday
2 Corinthians 3:12—4:2

"We have renounced disgraceful, underhanded ways; we refuse to practice cunning or to tamper with God's Word, but by the open statement of the truth we would commend ourselves to every man's conscience in the sight of God." (v. 2)

A young man was visiting with his pastor one afternoon. He had been in the pastor's confirmation class many years before. In fact, after his confirmation experience he rarely came to church except for Christmas and Easter. Now he was an adult and very much involved in the world. During this visit, he was bragging to his pastor about some of his business practices. He said, "In my business, I have lied many times in order to close certain deals. But it doesn't bother me. I don't care about that. If I have to cheat and steal, I will do it because I don't really care about that."

The pastor listened very intently to the young man's testimony. Then the pastor shared with him how Jesus had come to earth to die and be raised again so that his sins could be forgiven and so that he could have eternal life. At this point, the pastor asked the young man if he would do him a favor. Would he go home and look in the mirror and say ten times, "Jesus Christ died for me, but I don't care about that." The young man thought that it was a little silly but agreed that when he got home he would do that. When he got home, he began to do what the pastor had suggested. He looked in the mirror and said, "Jesus Christ died for me, but I don't care about that." He could only say it two times and then decided to return to the pastor's office at the church. With tears in his eyes he said, "If God sent his Son to die for me, I do care about that and I want to know more."

Source: Reprinted from *With Him All the Way* by Oscar Anderson, copyright 1948, Augsburg Publishing House. Used by permission of Augsburg Fortress.

14

Lent 1
Romans 10:8b-13

In a Danish village there was a Lutheran Church where each Sunday the people would walk into the church by way of the center aisle. At the front of the church, there was a break between the pews and a blank white wall. Every Sunday, the people of that church would walk down the center aisle to the front of the church and genuflect at the blank wall. A man visiting the church did not understand what the people were doing; when he asked them they said that they had always done this. Upon further investigation, he learned that hundreds of years before there had been a painting of the Virgin Mary on that wall. At the time of the Protestant Reformation when the church became Lutheran they had painted over the display of the Virgin Mary. Since the people had always bowed before the Virgin Mary, they just kept on bowing even though there was nothing there.

There are many people in church who simply go through the routine Sunday after Sunday. They know all the prayers by heart and could go through the entire service without ever opening the hymnal. For some that is all it has ever been. They do it because they have always done it that way before. But God wants to move beyond the routine. He wants the gospel to become so real that we confess with our own lips that Jesus is our Lord and Savior. God wants his love to be routine no longer but to be very real in our lives.

Source: Leith Anderson, *A Church for the 21st Century* (Minneapolis: Bethany House Publishers), p. 145. Used by permission.

15

Lent 2
Luke 13:31-35

In a small Swiss town there was a cathedral. It was called the Mountain Valley Cathedral. There has been a great deal of money spent on the wonderful stained-glass windows and tall arched ceiling. The cathedral also boasted of an outstanding pipe organ. The organ was designed in such a way that when it was played, people could hear it from all over the valley. As the people would work on their farms, they could often hear the organ as it was played. It gave great joy to the people of the valley for many decades.

Then one day the valley became silent. The organ was in need of repair. They called in one expert after another and yet no one was able to solve the problem. Specialists from all over Europe were asked to help and still no one was able to fix it.

Then one day when all hope was gone, an old man came to the cathedral. He asked if he could work on the organ. The sexton agreed and the old man worked for two days. The sexton was becoming nervous because the old man was saying nothing about what he was doing. Finally, on the third day, there was the sound of music all through the valley. People dropped what they were doing and ran to the cathedral. When the old man was done playing, the sexton asked why it was that he had been able to fix the organ after so many had failed. The old man said, "I am the one who built the organ, and I am the only one who can fix it."

This was the cry of Jesus as he looked over the city of Jerusalem. He wanted to fix the people but they would have nothing to do with him. The truth is that only the one who made us can fix us.

Source: *Parables, Etc.* (Platteville, Colorado: Saratoga Press), February 1987, p. 6. Used by permission.

16

Lent 3
Luke 13:1-9

"... unless you repent you will all likewise perish." (v. 5)

Most people think of AIDS as being transmitted sexually or through intravenous drug use. There are few actual cases of anyone contracting the virus in other ways. However, there is the case of two brothers. One of the brothers had advanced symptoms of AIDS. The other brother was not infected at all with the deadly disease. Then one day the two brothers got into a very violent fight. The infected brother continuously smashed his head against his brother's head. Both men bled a great deal into each other's exposed wounds. Soon after this episode the non-infected brother tested positive for the virus.

It is stories like these that have caused the medical community to revisit how they view sports. The Center for Disease Control did conduct one study a few years ago, reviewing eleven NFL teams playing 155 games. The scientists recorded 575 bleeding injuries. From this they calculated that the risk of getting AIDS on the field was 1 in 85 million. According to official records there has not been a case of transmission on the field to date.

However, minds were challenged again in the sport of boxing. In February of 1996, a boxer by the name of Tommy Morrison announced to the world that he is HIV-positive. It turns out that Tommy had been very active in areas beyond boxing. Because of his fame, which had also extended into some television appearances, Tommy was very attractive to a lot of women. Tommy soon discovered that he could have almost any woman he wanted at any time. Because of this philandering activity, Tommy became HIV-positive.

Tommy Morrison described himself and many others when he tried to explain how this could happen. Yes, he gave the normal reflection that he never thought that this could ever happen to him. No, he was not careful but instead very reckless. Perhaps he stated the situation best when he said, "I thought that I was bulletproof."

Wasn't that the problem that Jesus saw in the many arrogant religious leaders of his day? Isn't that our problem when we try to live lives that are distant from God? Couldn't we say along with Tommy Morrison, "I thought I was bulletproof"?

Source: *Time* (New York City: Time-Life Syndication), February 26, 1996, p. 59.

17

Lent 4
2 Corinthians 5:16-21

Walter Elias was born in the city; now his parents had just moved to the country. Walter loved being on the farm because it meant that he spent more time in the land of make-believe.

On this particular day in the middle of summer, Walter Elias decided to go exploring. Living on a farm meant that his parents were very busy and did not seem to mind that he was off playing, using that wonderful imagination of his. He went quite a way from the farmhouse to an apple orchard. When he got close to the orchard, to his absolute amazement, he saw sitting on a branch of one of the apple trees an owl. He just stood there and stared at the owl. He thought about what his father had told him about owls. His father had said that owls always rested during the day because they hunted throughout the night. This owl was definitely asleep. He also thought that this owl might make a great pet. So, he made up his mind that he would try to capture the bird and take it to the farmhouse and turn it into a pet.

Walter Elias began his careful creep toward the owl. He was careful not to make too much noise by stepping on branches or leaves. The owl must have been in a deep sleep because he never heard Walter Elias walking toward it. Finally, Walter was standing right under the owl. He reached up and grabbed the owl by the legs. Immediately, the owl was awakened and came to life. Any thought that Walter might have had of capturing the bird was quickly forgotten. The owl began to fight for its freedom as Walter held on so very tightly, probably because of fear.

The events that followed are difficult to explain. The owl fought violently and was screaming for its life. In his panic, Walter Elias, still holding on to the owl, threw it to the ground and stomped it to death. After things calmed down, Walter looked at the now dead and bloody bird and began to cry. He ran back to the farm and obtained a shovel and went back to the orchard to bury the owl.

Now at night he would dream of that owl. Even as an adult he would never really get over what had happened on that lazy summer day so long ago. Deep down it affected him for the rest of his life. Walter never, ever killed anything again. That seven-year-old boy was transformed by that event and, coupled with his imagination, was later able to turn a personal tragedy into a triumph. Some say that he eventually set all the animals free. For that young boy grew up to become someone you have probably heard of: Walter Elias ... Disney.

Radical transformation is what happened to the apostle Paul. He understood better than anyone how a leopard could change its spots. A transforming event happened to him as well on that road to Damascus, an event that would alter his life forever. As a result the world has never been the same either. Because of this one man, whose life was so dramatically changed by the Holy Spirit, the world was able to hear the good news of the gospel.

Source: Paul Harvey, *More of Paul Harvey's the Rest of the Story* (New York City: William Morrow & Company), p. 13.

18

Lent 5
Philippians 3:4b-14

"But whatever gain I had, I counted as loss for the sake of Christ." (v. 7)

There was a Scotsman whose wife became ill. At first it did not seem like anything serious. However, as time went on she became worse with each passing day. When she got really sick she asked her husband if she could have some help. Could they get word to the doctor or could he go into town and at least get some medicine for her? Each time she asked her husband, he would tell her to wait a little longer to see if perhaps she would get better on her own. At the root of the problem was the fact that he just did not want to give up any of his precious money. His money was of more value to him than even his wife's health and well-being.

Finally, after many days of her being sick, even the husband began to worry about her condition. He decided that it was time for him to make a trip into town and purchase the medicine that might help his wife get well. As he prepared to leave for town, he said to his wife, "I've put a candle in the window, and I'll be walking backwards to the apothecary shop. If you should feel yourself a-going, would you mind blowing out the candle?"

What do you value the most?

19

Passion/Palm Sunday
Philippians 2:5-11

Several years ago I had the occasion to meet A.C. Lyles. A.C. is a movie producer in Hollywood who was involved in such movies as *The Hunt for Red October*. He is also a great storyteller and the stories are usually true. A.C. is a very close friend to former President Ronald Reagan and can talk for hours about events in the White House that you never read about in the newspaper.

Among the many stories that I have heard him tell is the one about the waning days of the Reagan White House. A.C. was with President Reagan in the Oval Office having a friendly conversation. A.C. noticed that his friend the President was working on something and asked him what he was doing. The President told him that he was filling out the paperwork that would be needed for him to obtain a California driver's license when he returned home. A.C. couldn't believe what he was hearing or seeing. He asked the President why he thought that he needed a driver's license when he had not driven a car in years and when he would still be driven by the Secret Service when he did return home. President Reagan looked at his friend A.C. and said, "Well, I thought I might need it for identification."

Imagine being a two-term president and one of the most recognizable people in the world and still believing that you are just like anyone else. Paul encourages us to have the same mind as Christ, who saw himself as a servant.

20

Easter
1 Corinthians 15:19-26

There was a little boy who would always come home late from school. Even though his parents told him that they did not want him to do this, he would still be late in coming home from school. There was always something to distract the little boy. He would get into a dodgeball game after school with some other boys and would lose track of time and would come home late. His parents always worried about him. All they wanted him to do was come home from school first and then he could go out and play. They would explain to him that they only wanted to know that he was safe. After every explanation, he would promise to do better and each day he would be tempted away by friends on their bikes or by some local dog with whom he could play catch.

Finally, the day came when the parents decided that they had to take some kind of action. They told the boy that if he failed to do what they were asking, they would have to punish him. He seemed to understand. In fact, the next morning as he left for school, his mother reminded him that he had to come home right after school and he said that he would. When the last bell rang, he began his journey home, totally forgetting what his parents had asked of him. He got so involved in a game with some other boys that by the time he got home his father had already arrived home from work. The boy noticed that it was unusually quiet in the house so he went upstairs to play with his toys.

When he was called downstairs for dinner, he went over to the place where he usually sat and he could not believe his eyes. There on his plate was a slice of bread next to a glass of water. He stared at it for a while, realizing that this was his punishment for being late. Then his father reached over and took the plate with the slice of bread and replaced it with his own plate. His father's plate was filled with slices of roast beef and mashed potatoes covered with gravy. Throughout the rest of the meal, the boy ate the roast beef, while the father ate the slice of bread and drank the water.

Many years later when that boy became a man, he said that this experience taught him what God was really like. He is the one who would come and take our punishment. He is the one who would come to destroy death. Through the cross of Jesus and his resurrection, we too can learn what God is really like.

Source: *Dynamic Preaching,* Seven Word Corporation, September, 1996, p. 38. Used by permission.

21

Easter 2
John 20:19-31

A young couple fell in love in a very unique way. They had been corresponding by mail over a long period of time and simply fell in love with each other. What made it special was the fact that they had not exchanged pictures and so it was truly a mutual love of the person.

They finally decided that it was time for them to meet each other. They developed a plan by which they would meet at the airport. She said that she could be recognized because she would wear a green scarf, a green hat, and a green carnation pinned to her coat.

When the day arrived, the man got off the airplane and began looking for the woman in green. It did not take long for him to spot a woman wearing a green scarf, a green hat, and a green carnation. However, it did not take long either for him to realize how very unattractive this woman was. She was one of the worst-looking women he had ever seen. He did not know what to do next. Should he go over and talk to the woman or should he get back on the airplane and not make his presence known? He felt obligated to at least speak to her. So he walked over and greeted the woman and told her his name.

The woman instantly barked back at him and said, "I don't know what this is all about. I don't know you." She explained it all by saying, "That woman over there paid me $5.00 to wear this scarf and carnation." When he looked over to see who had paid the $5.00, he saw one of the most beautiful women he had ever seen. When the two loving pen pals were able to talk, she explained that all of her life men had wanted to be with her just because of her looks. She wanted someone who would love her just for who she was.

Too often we want proof before we will risk love. So much of the time our love is conditional. Jesus said to Thomas, "Have you believed because you have seen me? Blessed are those who have not seen and yet believe."

Source: *The Pastor's Story File* (Platteville, Colorado: Saratoga Press), July 1987, p. 7. Used by permission.

22

Easter 3
John 21:1-19

Since many of the followers of Jesus were fishermen, it made sense for Jesus to use fishing as an example of the Christian life. In Matthew 4:19, as Jesus is walking by the Sea of Galilee, he sees Simon Peter and Andrew in the process of fishing. He says to them, "Follow me, and I will make you fishers of men."

In this text, Jesus gives them another picture of the work they would be doing. On their own, they are not able to catch many fish, but when Jesus commands them to cast the net on the other side of the boat, they catch more fish than they can handle. How are we doing at catching fish? Perhaps the problem is that we keep doing it the same way and the Lord would like us to try a new method.

The apostle Paul in 1 Corinthians 9:22 says, "I have become all things to all men, that I might by all means save some." Maybe that's the same as casting your nets on the other side of the boat.

Several years ago when I was visiting Norway, the land of my great-grandparents, I learned something about evangelism. Since my wife was born in Norway, her family was giving us a tour of the country that on occasion was off the beaten track. On our way from Trondheim to the little island of Stord, we came across one of the famous Stave churches. These churches are around 1,000 years old. They are made of wood and are built with large posts or staves that go into the ground. At one time, there were around 1,000 Stave churches; now there are only thirty. One of the reasons is that the wood rots over time. However, the one that we saw had its posts in a rock foundation, and this explains why it is still in existence.

What was really fascinating to me were the symbols on the walls. I recognized most of them but there were some that I did not understand. I asked one of the guides what they meant. She told me that the symbols that I did not recognize were pagan symbols. It seems that when King Olaf became a Christian, he would go into the villages and demand that the people all become Christians. Since the Christian faith was forced on the people, they would display pagan symbols so as to meet the people where they were.

I am not suggesting that we use pagan symbols to reach our current society. However, we can do some things with music and in other areas that would better relate to our culture. If the Norwegians and the apostle Paul can learn that, certainly we can try to relate to our culture without destroying the gospel. Perhaps this is what Jesus meant by casting the net on the other side of the boat.

23

Easter 4
Revelation 7:9-17

"Then one of the elders addressed me, saying, 'Who are these, clothed in white robes, and whence have they come?' I said to him, 'Sir, you know.' And he said to me, 'These are they who have come out of the great tribulation; they have washed their robes and made them white in the blood of the Lamb.' " (vv. 13-14)

Violet Asquith was once sitting next to Winston Churchill at a dinner party. She said that he sat there for a long time and said very little. She reported that he seemed to be in deep thought. Then he became aware of his environment and began to recognize that she was there. At that point, he turned and asked her how old she was. She told him that she was nineteen years of age. He told her that he was 32 years old. Then he said, "Curse ruthless time! Curse our mortality. How cruelly short is the allotted span for all we must cram into it!" He then went on to speak at length about the shortness of life and ended by saying, "We are all worms. But I do believe that I am a glowworm."

Because of Jesus Christ, all who trust in him as Savior and Lord can make the same claim.

Source: William Manchester, *The Last Lion* (Boston: Little, Brown & Co.), p. 387.

24

Easter 5
John 13:31-35

"A new commandment I give to you, that you love one another; even as I have loved you, that you also love one another. By this all men will know that you are my disciples, if you have love for one another." (vv. 34-35)

There is a special hospital in London for those whom other hospitals consider a lost cause. It is a hospital for those who are diagnosed as "terminal."

Most people would consider such a hospital to be a very sad place, but it is not. Actually, it is a hospital filled with hope and a lot of life. The emphasis in this London hospital is on life and not on death. The truth is that several of the patients have seen remissions in the disease process instead of death. A great deal of the credit is given to the way the facility is run.

The basic philosophy is different from most other hospitals. In this program the patients are expected to give themselves away in service to the other patients. Each patient is given another patient for whom to care. So, for example, a person who is unable to walk might be given the task of reading to another who is blind. The blind person would then push the wheelchair of the one who could not walk but who gives directions on where to push the chair.

Is this not the new commandment to which Jesus referred? He calls us to be disciples who love one another. We are the ones who are healed and strengthened when we learn how to give and how to love.

Source: Bruce Larson, *Passionate People* (Dallas: Word Publishers), p. 203.

25

Easter 6
John 14:23-29

"But the Counselor, the Holy Spirit, whom the Father will send in my name, he will teach you all things...." (v. 26)

Henry Ford had a very important relationship with a man by the name of Charlie Steinmetz. Steinmetz was a very different man. To begin with, he was a dwarf and he was deformed. But there was something else about Charlie Steinmetz that was very important to Henry Ford. Steinmetz was truly a genius in the area of electrical engineering. It was Charlie Steinmetz who had built the first generators in the Ford plant in Dearborn, Michigan.

One afternoon those generators stopped running. The regular mechanics worked at solving the problem but simply failed. Every hour that the plant was not operating meant a financial loss for the Ford Motor Company. They decided that the only one who could solve their problem was Charlie Steinmetz. He was brought in to fix the generators.

This brilliant man worked for a short time and the generators were working again. Several days later Henry Ford got a bill for the work that was done. The bill was for $10,000, a lot of money in those days and especially for less than a day of work. Even though Ford was a very wealthy man he wrote Steinmetz a letter. He wrote, "Charlie, isn't this bill just a little high for a few hours of tinkering around on those motors?"

The bill came back with some modification which seemed to explain everything. Now it read, "For tinkering around on the motors: $10.00. For knowing where to tinker: $9,990.00. Total: $10,000.00." Henry Ford got the point and paid the bill.

Jesus promised his disciples that one was coming who would lead them into all truth. You could call him an expert and he is sent as a gift.

Source: *Parables, Etc.* (Platteville, Colorado: Saratoga Press), January 1990, p. 5. Used by permission.

26

Ascension Sunday
Luke 24:44-53

"And that repentance and forgiveness of sins should be preached in his name to all nations." (v. 47)

This is a story about two young men I once encountered. The first young man I met in a juvenile detention center. He was in jail for having killed his brother. Each time that I came to visit, we would talk about his life in jail and how things were going for him. We would talk about what he might do if he were not in jail. Then I worked up the courage to ask him why he had killed his brother. I thought the answer might be that his brother attacked him or something like that. Instead, he said that he had killed his brother because his brother slapped him in the face. I could not believe what I was hearing.

The other young man I met surprised me just as much. It seems that many years before I was the pastor of that congregation, this young man was a member. He had been an acolyte who would light the candles and help receive the offering. He came in to talk with me because he wanted me to know that when he was an acolyte he would steal money out of the offering trays. In fact, he had done this many times and felt badly about what he had done. He told me that he was now in Alcoholics Anonymous and working through his twelve steps and knew that he needed to make restitution. He said that he had calculated how much he had stolen and with interest how much money that would be. He handed me an envelope full of money and asked for my forgiveness.

What was the difference between these two young men? The difference was repentance. One found healing and wholeness while the other sat in jail. The difference was repentance.

27

Day Of Pentecost
John 14:8-17 (25-27)

"Peace I leave with you; my peace I give to you; not as the world gives do I give to you. Let not your hearts be troubled, neither let them be afraid." (v. 27)

Four centuries ago there was an incident that can serve as an example of the power of fear. It was the occasion of the last Tatar invasion of Russia in the fall of 1462. The two armies faced each other on the banks of the Oka River, which is located about 200 miles east of Moscow. For several days they had been engaged in battle. When the Tatar army would attempt to cross the Oka River, they would be beaten back by the Russians. It was the Oka River that gave the inferior Russian army any chance of surviving. After several days it began to appear that the river would be all the Russians needed to be saved from the onslaught of the Tatars. But then something happened that frightened them greatly. A cold wave developed that blew down the Ural Mountains and caused the Oka River to begin to freeze. If the river were to freeze over completely, it would mean that the Tatars would be able to cross and the Russians would be destroyed.

As the night passed the Russian soldiers were sitting by their fires discussing the problem of the freezing water. They knew full well what would happen if the enemy were able to cross on the hardened ice. With the wind growing stronger their fears evolved as well and by midnight the entire Russian army left their encampment. They did not stop until they had reached Moscow.

In the morning when the Tatars awakened they soon realized that the Russians were no longer on the other side of the river. They couldn't believe what they were seeing. This only caused the soldiers and their officers to speculate as to what might be happening. They concluded that the Russians had probably crossed the river many miles to the east and that they would now attack from the rear. Now it was the Tatars who were in a panic. In less than two hours they left their tents and were in retreat. The Tatars did not stop running until they reached the Volga River.

These two armies allowed fear, which was based in their imaginations, to lead and guide them. Too many times we function in the same way. We were built for faith and not fear. Jesus promises that the Holy Spirit will empower us in all that we do. Jesus promises that he will give us his peace and then we will not need to be afraid.

Source: William Stidger, *There Are Sermons in Stories* (New York City: Abingdon-Cokesbury Press), p. 154. Used by permission.

28

Trinity Sunday
John 16:12-15

"When the Spirit of truth comes, he will guide you into all the truth...." (v. 13)

Sometimes it is hard to determine just who is telling the truth. There are times when two people, who are for the most part very believable, are telling two different stories. Whom do you believe? How do you really know who is telling the truth?

During the last twenty years the lie detector business has been growing. While these tests are not used in court, they are being used more and more by businesses. Companies want to know if their employees are lying and/or stealing while in their employ.

In East India thousands of years ago those who were suspected of committing a crime were taken into a darkened room. There in that room with the suspect were only the person who would question them and a donkey. The suspect was asked to hold the donkey's tail and was told that the donkey would bray if he told a lie. What the suspect did not know was that the donkey's tail was covered with black soot. If the suspect was going to lie when questioned he would never touch the donkey's tail. The liar could always be identified as the one who walked out of the room with clean hands.

Source: Paul Harvey, *More of Paul Harvey's the Rest of the Story* (New York City: William Morrow & Company), p. 68.

29

Proper 6
Luke 7:36—8:3

College students are notorious for their laundry problems while away at college. This seems to be especially true for freshmen.

It is not uncommon, of course, for a student to put this task off for as long as possible. In fact, you can sometimes tell that students on campus will soon be dealing with their laundry when they start wearing the nicer clothing that they have. Sometimes they have been known to store up dirty clothes in anticipation of a visit home, where they just know that Mom will be more than happy to help out.

One college freshman went to the laundry room in his dorm with a pile of dirty clothes. They were all bundled together inside an old sweatshirt. He was so embarrassed by how dirty his clothes were that he did not want anyone to see them. He took the bundle of dirty clothes and without untying them stuffed them into the washer. When the machine stopped running he was delighted to find that they were still all tied together in one large knot. As he removed the bundle from the washer he kept them tied together as he placed the laundry into the dryer. After they had gone through the drying cycle he was even happier to find that the tied bundle was still intact. When he finally returned to his dorm room he quickly discovered that the clothes had certainly gotten wet and were dried but they were still dirty.

That is the same thing that happens to us when we fail to confess our sins. When we never admit to God our helplessness and our need for his power, we too keep the bundle all tied up. When we go to church and simply go through the routine we might get wet but we never really feel very clean. Only confession of our sins and faith in Christ can cleanse us from all our sins.

Source: Michael Green, editor, *Illustrations for Biblical Preaching* (Grand Rapids, Michigan: Baker Book House), p. 336.

30

Proper 7
Galatians 3:23-29

"Now before faith came, we were confined under the law, kept under restraint until faith should be revealed. So that the law was our custodian until Christ came...." (vv. 23-24a)

Some time ago there was a documentary on television about wildlife in their natural environment. This program showed a pregnant black bear chasing her cubs up a tree. She was growling at these two-year-old cubs who ran up the tree, not knowing their mother's purpose. After the cubs got to the top of the tree the mother left the scene. At first it appeared that perhaps she had left to go to obtain food for her cubs. Then it was speculated that the mother bear went off to protect her cubs from some invader. After some time it was revealed by the announcer that the truth of the matter was that this was how mother bears do parenting. She abandoned her cubs on purpose so that she could go and prepare for her unborn cubs. Her instincts told her that at two years her little cubs were ready to be on their own. In fact, after she had been gone for a while the cubs did come down from that tree. When they got on the ground they looked around, grunted, and then went about gathering berries.

This could never happen to human two-year-olds. If we were abandoned at that age we would have a difficult time getting over it all. If we survived, it would affect us for the rest of our lives. We are not built that way. We were created by God to be cared for and for someone to look after us.

Most often we see the law of God as only our nemesis in relation to forgiveness and grace. Shouldn't we also see the law as our caretaker and custodian?

Source: Patricia Love, *The Emotional Incest Syndrome* (New York City: Bantam Books), p. 119. Used by permission.

31

Proper 8
Galatians 5:1, 13-25

"But the fruit of the Spirit is love, joy, peace, patience, kindness, goodness, faithfulness, gentleness, self-control; against such there is no law." (vv. 22-23)

In the introduction to his book *Fruits of the Spirit*, Charles Hembree remembers an ancient fable. The fable tells of three merchants who were crossing the Arabian Desert. Because of the heat of the desert they were traveling at night. On that starless night they were crossing over a dry creek bed. As they were crossing a voice in the darkness spoke to them. The voice told them to stop right where they were. Then they were commanded to bend down and pick up the pebbles that were around them in the dry creek bed and put them in their pockets. After they did this they were told to leave and continue on their way and not to camp near the creek bed. The voice from the darkness continued to tell them that in the morning they would be both happy and sad.

Being very frightened by all of this, they traveled through the night and did not stop until they could see the sun. With the arrival of the morning they began to look in their pockets. Instead of finding pebbles in their pockets they found precious jewels. Yes, they were both happy and sad. They were happy that they had listened to the voice of the night but they were also sad that they did not pick up more pebbles.

Charles Hembree goes on to say: "This legend beautifully expresses how many feel about the unsearchable riches of God's Word. We are thrilled we have absorbed as much as we have, but sad because we have not absorbed much more." He goes on to say that this sentiment certainly applies to this verse in Galatians which describes the fruit of the Spirit. Perhaps we should also call these fruits the jewels of the Spirit.

Source: Charles Hembree, *Fruits of the Spirit* (Grand Rapids, Michigan: Baker Book House), p. 7.

32

Proper 9
Galatians 6:7-16

In India there is a tribe known as the Santals. Missionaries who work with them have observed many interesting characteristics about their lifestyle.

One of the more notable facts concerning the Santals is how they carry a burden. The women carry a burden on their heads while the men use a long pole. When a baby is born everyone asks, "Does he carry on the head or on the shoulder?" which is another way of asking if the child is a boy or a girl.

A missionary who works with the Santals once had a friend come for a visit. He asked a Santal to meet him and bring his luggage. The Santal, carrying pole in hand, went to retrieve the missionary's friend. When he got to the station he encountered a problem. The visitor only had one bag. The Santal's normal response would be to divide the burden in half and put the halves on each end of the pole and carry the burden. However, he could not divide this burden in half. So the Santal found a rock that weighed as much as the luggage bag. He tied the rock to one end of the pole and the luggage bag to the other and carried home the "doubled burden." He found that the double burden was lighter than the single bag of luggage.

When we live lives of selfishness we, too, will find it to be more difficult. When we become a giver instead of a taker we discover that life is easier and in fact lighter, for "whatever a man sows, that he will also reap."

Source: Stuart Robertson, *Balanced Burdens* (London: Hodder and Stoughtonl Limited), p. 9.

33

Proper 10
Luke 10:25-37

The story is told of the fourth wise man who had followed the Star announcing the birth of Jesus. He, too, went to Bethlehem with a gift for the Savior. His gift was that of precious jewels to give to Jesus.

On his way to Bethlehem he found a man who had been beaten and robbed by thieves and left to die. The wise man took the injured man to an inn and paid for his care with one of the jewels that had been meant for Jesus.

When he finally arrived in Bethlehem, Mary and Joseph had fled to Egypt with Jesus. He found that Herod and his soldiers were killing children and that Mary and Joseph had escaped with Jesus. The wise man saw a soldier preparing to kill one of the children of Bethlehem and so he bribed him with another jewel to save the child's life. The child's mother was relieved and very grateful.

The wise man went on to Egypt in pursuit of Jesus and his parents. However, while in Egypt the wise man became ill and a kind but poor woman nursed him back to health. On one occasion he found this woman crying and soon discovered why. Her son had been forced to join the army and now this woman was very distraught. The wise man was so grateful to this woman for all she had done that he used his last jewel and bought her son out of the army. Now he had nothing to offer Jesus.

Thirty years had passed and the wise man thought that he should return to his home. On his journey when he was passing through Jerusalem it was the day that Jesus was to be crucified. Upon learning this he stood with the crowd hoping that he still might see Jesus.

As he stood waiting to see Jesus, a tile from a nearby roof fell and landed on the wise man's head and killed him. Some might argue that his life was a failure because he never brought his gifts to Jesus. Yet, because he believed in Jesus as God's anointed, he was transported to heaven. There in heaven he finally saw Jesus. Jesus was on his throne and wearing a crown. The wise man could barely believe his eyes when he saw the crown of Jesus. For there in the center of the crown were the three jewels he had given to help others. "When we do it to the least we do it unto Jesus."

Source: Stuart Robertson, *Balanced Burdens* (London: Hodder and Stoughton, Limited), p. 142.

34

Proper 11
Luke 10:38-42

When Charles Dickens was a little boy he was unhappy and neglected, for he was working in a factory. During his dinner break he would walk the streets of London looking at everything.

Sometimes he would go to the coffee house on St. Martin's Lane. Years later he would tell how on one occasion he was sitting in this coffee house and looked up to see two words written on the glass door. These words created a great fear and panic within him. They were the words "Moor Eeffoc." He did not understand what they could mean. With his imagination he speculated that they might have something to do with the Moors. He knew what a Moor was. Could it be that something cruel and dangerous was behind those doors? Could it be some evil person who wanted to kill him? He simply sat there with his food growing cold wondering what it all meant.

Then it was time to leave. He knew that he would have to go through those ominous doors. With all of his courage he went through those potentially evil doors and when he looked back he discovered that the words on the door now read, "Coffee Room."

Apparently he had been reading the words backward on a glass door. Perhaps Martha had it backward, too.

Source: Stuart Robertson, *Balanced Burdens* (London: Hodder and Stoughton, Limited), p. 20.

35

Proper 12
Colossians 2:6-15

"See to it that no one makes a prey of you by philosophy and empty deceit, according to human tradition, according to the elemental spirits of the universe, and not according to Christ." (v. 8)

Two men were high up in a hot air balloon. The winds had been strong and they had been drifting for some time. As they were checking their maps and looking at the ground below, they were not able to get their bearings. They were hopelessly lost and did not know what to do.

Then one of the men had a great idea. "Let's lower the balloon down closer to the ground and try to find someone who can give us directions," he said. They both agreed that this was a great idea. After lowering the balloon they saw a man and started yelling at him, hoping to get his attention. Finally, the man noticed the two lost balloonists. They asked him if he knew where they were. "Why, yes, you are fifty feet high in a hot air balloon." One of the balloonists turned to the other and said, "Let's stop listening to these CPAs." "How do you know that he is a CPA?" asked the other. "Because he gave us perfectly accurate information that was of absolutely no value to us whatsoever."

Source: *Parables, Etc.* (Platteville, Colorado: Saratoga Press), December 1985. Used by permission.

36

Proper 13
Luke 12:13-21

One of the great struggles in our lives is the one that we have with materialism. Often our childhood affects the way we see money and possessions. In my own life, the fact that I had parents who were both products of the Great Depression shaped the way in which money is viewed. My parents always lived as if they would be poor again. As a result, it has sometimes been difficult to see money as a tool and not the end result.

In my first congregation, we were discussing a maintenance project that was going to cost a large sum of money. Everyone was just a little nervous about the project because of the cost. Then one of our members, Larry Brown, said something that I have always remembered. Larry said, "It is only money." He was right. It was not our lives or our health that we were discussing, but only money. It was a liberating word to us all. That comment helped me to understand a lot better the idea that money is simply a tool that we are to possess and not to own.

Abraham Lincoln was once walking down the street with two boys. Each of the boys was crying and was terribly upset. Someone shouted over to Abe and asked what was wrong with those two boys. He said, "The same thing that is wrong with the rest of the world. I have one walnut and each boy wants it." The sooner we learn that the things that we have are a gift from God to use and not to own, the better off we will be.

37

Proper 14
Hebrews 11:1-3, 8-16

My good friend and former professor Dr. James Kallas, in his days at California Lutheran University, used to tell a story from his youth. He would tell the story to teach us the Jewish understanding of faith and how they saw everything as the will of God.

When Jim was a young man he worked in a warehouse for a Jewish man. One day the man asked him to go up to the fourth floor and put a refrigerator on a dolly and bring it down the elevator. Jim did just as he had been told. He put the refrigerator on the dolly and delivered it to the elevator. He pushed the dolly and refrigerator into the elevator and then he heard a loud crash. It seems that the elevator was not where it was supposed to be and the refrigerator fell down the shaft to the floor, smashing into hundreds of pieces. To say the least, Jim was glad that he wasn't backing into the elevator.

After all the noise had subsided the owner of the warehouse came running over to see what had happened. He looked around and saw all the broken pieces. The refrigerator could never be repaired. The man looked up to Jim and said, "God has spoken. Go get another refrigerator."

38

Proper 15
Hebrews 11:29—12:2

"... *let us also lay aside every weight, and sin which clings so closely, and let us run with perseverance the race that is set before us, looking to Jesus the pioneer and perfecter of our faith....*" (vv. 1b-2a)

In Plato's *Symposium* there is an allegory that imagines the beginning of human beings. The gods created humans in a very unique way. Each human was a mixture of both male and female. In other words, each human had four hands, two noses, four feet, and two mouths. They also had both male and female genitals. Having been created in this way they were extremely powerful. They were so powerful that they became aggressive against the gods. Fearing that they would try to take over, the gods decided that they must punish the humans. They decided that they could not kill the humans, for then there would be no one to worship them. Finally, Zeus decided that humans would continue to live but that they would be cut in half. By cutting them into two parts they would no longer retain the power. Zeus then went ahead with his plans and cut the humans in two, asking Apollo to help so that the wounds would not be apparent. After this was done the humans were sent separately in different directions into the world. These humans spent the rest of their lives searching for their other halves who could make them whole.

Some today live as if this story is true. Many spend their lives believing that another human being can fill the emptiness in their lives and make them whole. No other human being can make us whole. The songs on the radio are wrong. It will never work. Instead, we should "lay aside" this frivolous pursuit and all the other ones that never truly fulfill and look to Jesus. He is the only one who can satisfy our hunger for wholeness.

Source: Plato, *The Symposium.*

39

Proper 16
Hebrews 12:18-29

"... and to Jesus, the mediator of a new covenant, and to the sprinkled blood that speaks more graciously than the blood of Abel." (v. 24)

During World War II the Red Cross would provide blood for wounded soldiers. They had a practice of giving the name of the donor to the recipient so that the soldier could write and thank the donor if he should desire.

The Red Cross also had a policy that the blood that was given would be made available to anyone who would need it. That meant that even enemy soldiers could have the blood to save their lives.

Because the names of the donors were available, the medics developed a custom when the blood was needed for a Nazi officer. When a Nazi officer needed blood the medics would find a bottle of blood whose donor had a Jewish name. They would tell the Nazi that they had the blood that was needed to save his life. Then they would tell him that the blood was from a Jewish donor. Most of the Nazi officers would receive the blood but there were some who absolutely refused to receive it into their veins.

Source: *Parables, Etc.* (Platteville, Colorado: Saratoga Press), June 1985. Used by permission.

40

Proper 17
Hebrews 13:1-8, 15-16

"Do not neglect to show hospitality to strangers, for thereby some have entertained angels unawares." (v. 2)

One summer a farmer named Worthy Taylor hired a young man by the name of Jim to work the farm. Jim had many chores to perform each day. He had to milk the cows and chop the wood. Even though he ate with the family in the farmhouse he slept in the hayloft of the barn. During that summer he got to know and fell in love with the farmer's daughter. He eventually worked up enough courage to ask Farmer Taylor if he could marry the farmer's daughter. Worthy Taylor rejected the request because Jim did not have any money or any real future. So Jim decided to pack up his few belongings and leave.

Thirty-five years passed. During those years Worthy Taylor did very well. His net worth had grown considerably. He was doing so well that he decided that he should build a new barn. During the process of tearing down the old barn Farmer Taylor was looking at the rafters of the old barn. There above the place where Jim had slept some 35 years before was carved Jim's full name: "James A. Garfield." That name meant something to Taylor because Jim was now the President of the United States. Unaware, Worthy Taylor had opened his home to a future president.

Source: Bruce Larson, *My Creator, My Friend* (Dallas: Word Publishers), p. 101.

41

Proper 18
Luke 14:25-33

"So therefore, whoever of you does not renounce all that he has cannot be my disciple." (v. 33)

A man was once put in a dark cave. He was sentenced to die in the cave unless he could find his way out. The cave was 100 yards by 100 yards and he was told that there really was a way out.

The cave was sealed by a very large rock. After the cave was sealed the prisoner was allowed to take off his blindfold. In the midst of the darkness he walked around the cave. He had food, but it was bread and water which would only last for thirty days. The food was lowered to him from a hole in the ceiling of the cave which was about eighteen feet high. The opening was only one foot in diameter.

The man investigated the cave and soon discovered that there was a pile of rocks. He quickly determined that if he could build up the pile of rocks even higher, perhaps he could escape. By calculating both his height and his reach he believed that he needed to build the mound ten feet high.

Every moment was devoted to finding rocks and placing them in the pile. After two weeks he had built the mound to about six feet. He figured that over the next two weeks he could complete the task before the food would run out. He had not taken into account that he had already used up most of the rocks in the cave. Now he would have to use the rocks that were left and certainly more dirt. He had nothing with which to dig but his bare hands. After the next two weeks had passed he had only built the mound to nine-and-a-half feet; he thought that he could perhaps reach the opening if he were to jump. At this point he was near exhaustion.

As he tried to jump and reach the opening he fell. Now he was too weak to get up and try again and in two days he was dead.

When they came to remove his body from the cave, they removed the large stone that covered the entrance, and the light that poured in revealed everything. In the light it was evident that there was an opening in the wall of the cave at ground level. The hole in the wall was the beginning of a tunnel that traveled for 200 feet and led to freedom. The captured man had so focused on the opening above that he never thought that there could be another way out of the cave. The opening was right next to the mound that he had been building. The trouble was that the opening on the ground level was in the darkness and did not seem possible to him.

Too often people reject Jesus as a way to freedom because it seems too easy or impractical. Sometimes he is rejected because it seems too dark and difficult as in this verse. We think that we can do it by our own efforts and that we do not even need his help. Today he asks us to let go of all of our attempts to find freedom and follow him.

Source: John Bradshaw, *Healing the Shame that Binds* (Deerfield Beach, Florida: Health Communications, Inc.), p. 117. Used by permission.

42

Proper 19
Luke 15:1-10

"Now the tax collectors and sinners were all drawing near to hear him. And the Pharisees and the scribes murmured, saying, 'This man receives sinners and eats with them.'" (v. 1)

From time to time I have, as most pastors do, a conversation with someone about his or her relationship with God. Most often it is during pre-baptism or pre-marital counseling. Quite often it becomes rather apparent that while these people believe in God they feel very far from him. For many there is a certain amount of fear in their understanding of how God wants to relate to them. It then is my joy to share with them how the incarnate God came to die so that they might be forgiven and receive eternal life. At this point it is my prayer that they will hear this as good news. I try to help them see that they can move from religion to a living relationship with God through Jesus Christ. For some it seems too good to be true. They remain locked in with a distant faith that doesn't change their reality.

One of my pastor friends, Ray Farness, said many years ago in a sermon, "Though vicarious suffering saved us, vicarious faith will not do us any good." Instead, Ray says, we must become like the little girl who came home from church and told her mother that the pastor had spoken about her in his sermon. She said that in fact the pastor had read her name from the Bible. The mother couldn't really believe what she was hearing, so she asked her daughter what verse the pastor had read. She said that it was that verse that says, "Jesus receives sinners and 'edith' with them." We should all hear him speak our names and believe that the gift of the cross is just for us.

Source: Reprinted from *By the Obedience of One* (Minneapolis: Augsburg Publishing House), p. 80.

43

Proper 20
1 Timothy 2:1-7

"... who desires all men to be saved and to come to the knowledge of the truth." (v. 4)

One Sunday morning on a subway car in New York City people were traveling in relative peace and calm. They were reading their newspapers and were daydreaming out the window. At one stop the door opened and in stepped a man and his children. Instantly the peace and calm were destroyed by the behavior of the children. The children were running up and down the aisle. They were throwing things and screaming at the same time. The calm of a few minutes earlier was now absolute chaos.

To make matters even worse, the father of the children was not even aware of the upset that his children were causing. He just sat there staring out the window as if nothing were wrong. Finally, one of the passengers could not take it anymore. Someone had to do something. So the passenger got up and went over to the father of the children and said, "Sir, your children are causing a great deal of turbulence on this car. Do you think that you could try to control them?" Upon hearing those words the man came to life and responded, saying, "I am so sorry. I will try to calm them. We just came from the hospital. You see, their mother died this morning and they probably don't know what to do." Immediately, the passenger's attitude changed dramatically. What was it that changed his outlook? It was the truth. Because of the truth he moved from anger and hostility to an attitude of compassion and mercy. Truth changes everything.

Source: Stephen Covey, *The Seven Habits of Highly Effective People* (New York City: Simon & Schuster), p. 30.

44

Proper 21
1 Timothy 6:6-19

"For we brought nothing into the world, and we cannot take anything out of the world." (v. 7)

We are often afraid to speak of money in the church. We are concerned that someone will become offended. We do not want to confirm the position held by many that all the church wants is your money. As a result, we respond to this perception in a variety of ways. I know of one church that prints in its Sunday bulletin that visitors to the church are not expected to give financially but that this is the responsibility of the members of that church. I know of another church where the pastor announces that they only speak about giving once a year and that he as the pastor does not know what anyone in the church gives. We are very touchy on the subject and we find that we do not speak of it very often. Generally speaking, our response for most of the year is basic silence on the subject of money.

Yet Jesus is not silent on the subject, nor is the Bible. Perhaps that is because money seems to represent our priorities and what we consider important. A quick glance at our checkbook says a great deal about our lives. Our checkbook is probably more revealing than even a diary would be concerning our priorities. Too often we could be accused of putting more trust in our money than we do in God. We often see our bank account or investments as the vehicle for protecting our future. This is why the Bible is not silent on the subject.

When Charlemagne, the Frankish king, died, the people dealt with it in a unique fashion. Instead of the normal burial, using a shroud, they used his royal robe. They placed his royal robe on him and had him sitting on his throne for all to see. Then they placed a Bible on his lap. They had the Bible open with the King's forefinger on his right hand pointing at a particular Bible verse. The verse was Matthew 16:26: "For what will it profit a man, if he gains the whole world and forfeits his life?"

Source: Chevis Horne, *Basic Bible Sermons on Christmas* (Nashville: Broadman Press, 1991), p. 100. All rights reserved. Used by permission.

45

Proper 22
2 Timothy 1:1-14

"... our Savior Christ Jesus, who abolished death and brought life and immortality to light through the gospel." (v. 10b)

A pastor was preaching one of his first sermons in the new church to which he had been called. He did not know too many people yet. He was still in the process of learning names and who was related to whom. He was in the early stages of accessing the congregation and its needs.

As he was preaching he announced both a biblical truth and a certainty of reality. The pastor said, "Everyone in this congregation is going to die." After he said this he noticed that a man in the front row was laughing very robustly. The pastor couldn't believe his eyes. He stopped the sermon at this point and said to the man, "Sir, I just told the people in this congregation that they are going to die, and you are laughing. Why are you laughing?" The man in the front row composed himself a little and responded by saying, "I am not a member of this congregation."

Source: *Parables, Etc.* (Platteville, Colorado: Saratoga Press), August 1985, p. 5. Used by permission.

46

Proper 23
Luke 17:11-19

I have noticed that at Thanksgiving time it is difficult for people to give God thanks and praise. You hear people say on that day that they are grateful but that is where it ends. They rarely direct their thankfulness to God. One year my daughter's school had a Thanksgiving day program for the parents. I was so saddened that during the program all they could sing about was "Tom Turkey." You would have thought that it was a poultry holiday.

Not only is it difficult for us to give thanks, but it seems that we can not graciously receive thanks. If we listen carefully to various conversations we will notice that sometimes someone will say, "Thank you," only to have the other person say, "No, thank you." Obviously, giving thanks has become a meaningless exercise for many people. We have reduced it to the level of telling one another to "have a nice day." This is nothing new; in our text Jesus was having the same problem.

So was one young mother who was preparing a dinner party at her home. She had spent all day in preparations for the big event. She was nervous and wanted everything to be just right for her guests. She had cleaned the house from top to bottom, polished the silver, arranged the flowers, and even made little name cards for each guest. Finally, the guests arrived and were eventually seated at the dinner table. The young mother turned to her daughter and asked her to offer the prayer. The daughter said that she did not know what to pray. "Just pray what Mommy would pray," the mother said. The little girl thought for a moment and then prayed, "Dear Lord, why did I invite all these people to dinner?"

47

Proper 24
2 Timothy 3:14—4:5

"For the time is coming when people will not endure sound teaching, but having itching ears they will accumulate for themselves teachers to suit their own likings, and will turn away from listening to the truth and wander into myths." (vv. 3-4)

In 1899 four Denver journalists encountered one another in the Denver railway station. Al Stevens, Jack Tournay, John Lewis, and Hal Wilshire represented the four newspapers in town and were sent by their editors to find a good story for the Sunday paper. They were all hoping that someone important would arrive at the station or that something interesting would happen so that they could write a great story. After the last train they decided to go over to the Oxford Hotel and have a beer.

Al stated that he was going to make up a story. At first no one took him seriously but then the idea grew. As a group they talked about the idea of writing individual phony stories. Soon they realized that they would probably get caught unless they all wrote the same story about something that was rather significant. After another round of beer the idea really began to develop. A domestic story could be rather quickly checked for its truth. So it was decided that they would write an international story. They thought that China was far enough away. They would write about China.

John came up with the ultimate story. A group of American engineers was traveling through Denver on their way to China. The Chinese government was taking estimates on tearing down the Great Wall. The Chinese wanted to tear down the wall because they wanted to send a message around the world that they welcomed foreigners and foreign trade. They wanted the world to know that they were not isolationists. These American engineers would be one of the groups that would bid on the job.

At 11 p.m. the details of the story were worked out. The four men, not wanting to leave anything to chance, went to the Windsor Hotel and registered four fictitious names to the hotel registry. They told the clerk to tell anyone who wanted to know that four engineers were passing through Denver on their way to China.

The next morning all four of the Denver papers carried the story on the front page. The headline on the *Times* stated it very clearly: "GREAT CHINESE WALL DOOMED! PEKING SEEKS WORLD TRADE!" To the absolute surprise of the journalists, the story was not only on the front page of their papers but it was also taken very seriously around the world and especially in China.

When the Chinese heard that the Americans were coming to destroy their national symbol they became angry. There was a group of Chinese who were very worried about foreign involvement in their country. This group attacked the embassies in Peking, killing hundreds of missionaries. Two months later 12,000 troops from six different countries invaded China for the reason of protecting their own citizens. All of this bloodshed became known as the Boxer Rebellion.

Source: Paul Harvey, *More of Paul Harvey's the Rest of the Story* (New York City: William Morrow & Company), p. 136.

48

Proper 25
2 Timothy 4:6-8, 16-18

"So I was rescued from the lion's mouth. The Lord will rescue me from every evil and save me for his heavenly kingdom. To him be the glory for ever and ever." (vv. 17b-18)

Norman Cousins wrote a book several years ago titled *Head First: the Biology of Hope*. In this book he describes his work at UCLA, where he worked with doctors and researchers concerning the effects of hope on patients in the hospital. One interesting experiment helps us to understand the power of hope in the healing process. In his research he discovered the work of Dr. J.W.L. Fielding, of the Department of Surgery at Queen Elizabeth Hospital in Birmingham, England. He conducted an experiment where 411 patients were told that they would experience hair loss as a result of chemotherapy which they were soon to receive. However, thirty percent of those patients received only a placebo and no chemotherapy and still experienced hair loss. Even when the pills they took had absolutely no medication their bodies still reacted as if they had had chemotherapy.

In another experience Normal Cousins records the true story of a young mother of three children who had cancer of the lung. Her children were ages four, six, and nine. Her cancer was not responding to treatment and her husband was told that she would probably not live very long. The husband flew his own mother out to California from Michigan to help him care for the children. At first the children were protected from the bad news, but as their mother's condition worsened the situation was explained to them.

For two months she stood at death's door. It seemed as if any day she would die. Then, due to some unique treatments, she began to recover. The tumors began to shrink. She quickly began to recover and was sent home to live.

At home she discovered a situation that she had probably never imagined. Her children did not know how to receive her. Her four-year-old said, "Mommy, Grandma said you were going to die. Why didn't you die?" The woman's mother-in-law did not welcome her home with great joy after having closed up her home in Michigan. The mother-in-law most likely expected to begin a new life of caring for her son and grandchildren. Even the husband did not know exactly what to say. His encouragement was not believable. The neighbors who had been so supportive now acted as if they had wasted their time or at least were premature in their caregiving. As a result the woman went into depression. It was not too long before the cancer began to recur. The renewed treatments did nothing to arrest the cancer and the woman died within two weeks of reentering the hospital.

If our bodies respond to negativity and despair, just imagine how they would respond to hope. We were designed by God to be people of hope and faith.

Source: Norman Cousins, *Head First: the Biology of Hope* (New York City: E.P. Dutton), pp. 106 and 230. Copyright 1989 by Norman Cousins. Used by permission of Dutton Signet, a division of Penguin Books U.S.A., Inc.

49

All Saints' Day
Ephesians 1:11-23

"... having the eyes of your hearts enlightened, that you may know what is the hope to which he has called you, what are the riches of his glorious inheritance in the saints, and what is the immeasurable greatness of his power in us who believe, according to the working of his great might which he accomplished in Christ when he raised him from the dead and made him sit at his right hand in the heavenly places." (vv. 18-20)

There was a king who held court every day. He would sit on his throne wearing his robe and crown as the people of his country would come to him stating their needs and requests. Each day, in addition to all the people who would come to the throne, there was also a holy man dressed in a beggar's robe who would come to the king. The holy man would hand the king a piece of fruit which the king would receive and then hand over to one of his assistants. Then the holy man would leave without ever saying a word to the king. This went on for many months and even years.

Then one day something happened that no one expected. No one knew that a monkey had gotten loose in the palace. When the holy man presented his gift of fruit to the king, the monkey jumped up on the stage and grabbed the fruit out of the hand of the king. Then the monkey took a bite out of the fruit and all were amazed at what they saw, because precious jewels fell out of the fruit. The king quickly turned and asked his assistant what he had been doing with the fruit. The assistant said that they had been throwing the fruit through the window of a locked room. When they opened the door of that room they found among the rotten and decaying fruit a fortune in jewels.

So much of the time we fail to take the grace of God seriously. Perhaps because it is a free gift that comes to us in the form of a cross it does not seem very valuable. Let us pray that God will give us a new understanding of his grace and mercy in Jesus Christ.

Source: William A. Miller, *Make Friends with Your Shadow* (Minneapolis: Augsburg Publishing House), p. 128. Used by permission.

50

Proper 27
2 Thessalonians 2:1-5, 13-17

One day late in the afternoon a missionary in Africa had a surprise visit. When he entered his small hut he discovered a very large python on the floor. He left the hut and went to his truck and retrieved his .45-caliber pistol. Even though he had his gun, he still had one important problem. He only had one bullet left in the gun. He could not afford to miss. All of his skill would be required in order to rid his hut of this deadly creature. If he missed, there was no telling what would happen next.

He took careful aim and pulled the trigger. He shot the python in the head. The python, which would soon die, was at this point only wounded in the head. It still had some life and some fight within itself. The python began to throw itself violently about. The missionary left the room and listened for some time as the python broke furniture and destroyed lamps and other personal items as it unleashed one last burst of energy. After some time things got quiet and the missionary assumed that the snake was dead. When he went back into his hut he found the snake dead and his home in shambles.

This is often the case with the enemies of God. The victory has been won in Jesus Christ and until his return the battle continues. Let us rejoice in the knowledge that Christ has won the battle.

Source: Dr. James Dobson, *When God Doesn't Make Sense* (Wheaton, Illinois: Tyndale House Publishers, Inc.), p. 194. Used by permission.

51

Proper 28
2 Thessalonians 3:6-13

Sometimes people do not think that their work is very important or significant. They go through each day believing that what they do is of little value or importance. They need to see the larger picture and how their job fits into the bigger picture. They need to discover, as Martin Luther said, the ministry of vocation.

During World War II, Winston Churchill as Prime Minister was traveling around his country. He was trying to motivate and inspire his fellow citizens. He was willing to go almost anywhere to encourage people in the war effort. He would, of course, always visit the troops. But he also visited those who worked on the farms and in the factories. He knew that the odds against them were great and that he must continue to help keep the morale high.

There was one group he had not yet seen. It was the coal miners. Someone asked him if he would be willing to see these men, who spend most of their time below the ground in such dangerous conditions. One man told Churchill that the miners did not feel that they were doing very much in the effort against the Nazis. He said that no one ever gave them any credit for the work that they did. Would he visit them, he asked. The Prime Minister told the man that he would be pleased to visit these men.

When Churchill visited the coal miners they were absolutely amazed that he was there. They could not believe that he would come to see them. All they could do was to stare with their dirty faces at the man who would lead Britain to victory. His words will never be forgotten by those who heard him on that day. "We will be victorious!" he said. "We will preserve our freedom. And years from now when our freedom is secure and peace reigns, your children and your children's children will come and they will say to you, 'What did you do to win our freedom in that great war?' And one will say, 'I marched with the Eighth Army!' Someone else will proudly say, 'I manned a submarine.' And another will say, 'I guided the ships that moved the troops and the supplies.' And still another will say, 'I doctored the wounds!' " The men sat with rapt attention wondering what he might say about them. "They will come to you," he shouted, "and you will say with equal right and equal pride, 'I cut the coal! I cut the coal that fueled the ships that moved the supplies! That's what I did. I cut the coal!' "

Source: Robert Schuller, *Be an Extraordinary Person in an Ordinary World* (Old Tappan, New Jersey: Fleming H. Revell), p. 89.

52

Christ The King
Luke 23:33-43

"And he said, 'Jesus, remember me when you come into your kingdom.' And he said to him, 'Truly, I say to you, today you will be with me in Paradise.'" (vv. 42-43)

In Toledo, Spain, there is an old cathedral. Visitors to the cathedral are told about a cardinal who is buried there. Tourists are directed to a side altar where the cardinal is buried in the floor. Just over the grave, a cardinal's hat is fastened to the ceiling. Since his burial a legend has developed about the cardinal and his hat. The legend states that when the hat falls from the ceiling to the floor, this will indicate that the soul of the cardinal has entered heaven. The only problem is that the hat has been hanging in the cathedral for 400 years.

What good news our Lord gives us! We don't have to wait 400 years to spend eternity with him. The promise is that "today" we can have eternal life. We don't have to worry that we have done enough to earn our way. He has made the way possible through his death, burial, and resurrection. If he can make this promise to the one dying next to him, certainly it applies to you as well. "Today is the day of salvation."

Source: John Brokhoff, *Grace Words From The Cross* (Lima, Ohio: CSS Publishing Co., Inc.), p. 17. Used by permission.

Topical Index

Topic	Page	Topic	Page
Advice	62	Motivation	20
Angels	66		
		No Waiting	84
Blood of Christ	65	Nurturing	53
Cheap Grace	79	Prayer	74
		Purpose	56
Denial of Death	70, 73		
Devil	81	Repentance	29, 32, 34, 48, 52
Evangelism	26, 42	Resurrection	28, 44
Evil	81	Ritual	30
Faith	69	Sacrifice	57
Fear	16, 49, 59	Salvation	84
Finding the Way	46, 84	Self-Denial	11, 13, 23, 56, 67
Forgiveness	25, 52		
Fruit of the Spirit	54	Self-Sufficiency	31
		Service	11, 45, 56
Grace	38, 84	Stewardship	20, 36, 61, 71
Greed	26, 36, 61		
		Transformation	34
Hope	21, 77	Truth	46, 51, 60, 70
Incarnation	15, 38, 40	Unconditional Love	38
		Victory	28, 84
Lie	75	Vocation	82
Lost	60		
Love	11, 63	Witness	12, 26
		Work	82

Scriptural Index

New Testament	Page	New Testament	Page
Matthew		**Acts**	
2:1-12	18	8:14-17	20
Luke		**Romans**	
1:39-45	15	10:8b-13	30
3:1-6	12		
3:7-18	13	**1 Corinthians**	
5:1-11	26	12:12-31a	23
7:36—8:3	52	13:1-13	25
10:25-37	57	15:12-20	28
10:38-42	59	15:19-26	38
12:13-21	61		
13:1-9	32	**2 Corinthians**	
13:31-35	31	3:12—4:2	29
14:25-33	67	5:16-21	34
15:1-10	69		
17:11-19	74	**Galatians**	
23:33-43	84	3:23-29	53
24:44-53	48	5:1, 13-25	54
		6:7-16	56
John			
2:1-11	21	**Ephesians**	
13:31-35	45	1:11-23	79
14:8-17 (25-27)	49		
14:23-29	46	**Philippians**	
16:12-15	51	2:5-11	37
20:19-31	40	3:4b-14	36
21:1-19	42		

New Testament	Page
Colossians	
2:6-15	60
3:12-17	16
1 Thessalonians	
3:9-13	11
2 Thessalonians	
2:1-5, 13-17	81
3:6-13	82
1 Timothy	
2:1-7	70
6:6-19	71
2 Timothy	
1:1-14	73
3:14—4:5	75
4:6-8, 16-18	77
Hebrews	
11:1-3, 8-16	62
11:29—12:2	63
12:18-29	65
13:1-8, 15-16	66
Revelation	
7:9-17	44

www.ingramcontent.com/pod-product-compliance
Lightning Source LLC
Chambersburg PA
CBHW071733040426
42446CB00012B/2347